ALASKA NATIVE GAMES

and How to Play Them

TWENTY-FIVE CONTESTS
THAT SURVIVED THE AGES

T0345119

TRICIA NUYAQIK BROWN // JONI KITMIIQ SPIESS

PHOTOGRAPHY BY ROY JAZHGUQ CORRAL

Foreword by NICK ILIGUTCHIAK HANSON, ESKIMO NINJA

Dedicated to Sheila Randazzo,
whose love for the athletes and
the games has nurtured healing,
and saved many.

**Turnagain Arm sunset,
Anchorage, Alaska.**

A PLACE TO SHINE

Athletes across the Far North train and compete locally as they prepare for these big events:

GREENLAND

Nuuk

Iqaluit

Shefferville

Newfoundland and Labrador

Quebec

Ontario

ARCTIC WINTER GAMES

Biennial

Past Host Locations:

ALASKA
Chugiak and Eagle River
Fairbanks
Kenai Peninsula

ALBERTA, CANADA
Grande Prairie
Hay River and Pine Point
Slave Lake
South Slave Region

GREENLAND
Nuuk

NORTHWEST TERRITORIES, CANADA
Wood Buffalo (Fort McMurray)
Yellowknife

NUNAVUT, CANADA
Iqaluit

QUEBEC, CANADA
Shefferville

YUKON TERRITORY, CANADA
Whitehorse

JUNIOR NATIVE YOUTH OLYMPICS

Annually
Hosted by Cook Inlet Tribal Council
1st-6th grades; Natives and non-Natives
Anchorage, Alaska

NATIVE YOUTH OLYMPICS

Annually since 1971
Hosted by Cook Inlet Tribal Council
7th-12th grades; Natives and non-Natives
Anchorage, Alaska

WORLD ESKIMO-INDIAN OLYMPICS

Annually since 1961
Native participants only
Fairbanks, Alaska

CONTENTS

Iñupiat drums. Native singing, drumming, and dancing are a social highlight during the Games.

PART I // ANCIENT GAMES AND MODERN MUSCLE

PART II // JUST AS FIERCE, BUT NEARLY FORGOTTEN

Nick Hanson competed in the traditional Native Games before and while he was a star on NBC's *American Ninja Warrior.*

FOREWORD
THE VALUE OF PLAYING GAMES

by Nick Iligutchiak Hanson

Across the country, fans of the NBC show *American Ninja Warrior* know me as the "Eskimo Ninja." We Ninjas follow a demanding course that requires balance, strength, endurance, and focus, the same attributes required to play the Alaska Native Games of my ancestors: Seal Hop, Eskimo Stick Pull, Blanket Toss, and more. Our Games are a bridge from the past that helps us find the best in ourselves and each other. If it weren't for World Eskimo-Indian Olympics (WEIO) and Native Youth Olympics (NYO), I wouldn't be where I am today.

Growing up in Unalakleet, a small town in western Alaska, I was beat up and bullied because I'm half Iñupiaq and half mixed European. So I don't necessarily look like I'm Alaska Native. They would call me "White Boy" and tell me "You shouldn't be here." Sometimes I was depressed, thinking things would never change.

Once I got pushed into a pile of dirt, and a boy named Axel Johnson threw a rock at my face. He actually broke my front tooth. Washing up at home, I looked at my reflection. *What is it gonna take to make this stop?* I thought. *Who am I and what am I passionate about?* I decided I wasn't going to let it affect me. I said, *I'm going to join sports.*

So I tried everything I could: cross-country running, volleyball, basketball. Everything except NYO. See, you can join as a seventh-grader and compete against the best in the world. But I didn't join until I was a junior.

Why? It was the *Native* Games; I figured these boys didn't want me on their *Native* team. But basketball and those other "conventional" sports were fine.

But when I was a junior, the captain of my basketball team said, "Hey, you should try out for WEIO and NYO. I'll teach you everything I know. You should come to practice." He begged me to join. "Whatever it takes, I'll teach you so you can get good enough to compete with me at state." He took me under his wing and taught me Scissor Broad Jump, One-Hand Reach, and Seal Hop. The first Games I played were the One-Foot and Two-Foot High Kick. He taught me all of the Games, and all his tricks.

I learned that every game had a value and a purpose. Seal Hop shows the hunting technique our ancestors used on the ice. They would get as low as they could on their fists, with a harpoon on their back and a sealskin over them. They'd hop and get close before jumping up and striking the seal. After it was harpooned, the seal would drop away, but the harpoon would stay across the ice hole and the sinew line would get taut. The hunter would grab that stick and pull, like what we do in Eskimo Stick Pull. Next they'd be kneeling on the ice to butcher their seal. If the ice broke off, they'd have to jump up quickly and run back to safety. And that's the Kneel Jump.

All of these skills required every ounce, every muscle, every tendon to be in good shape. It's the original cross-fit workout. And you've got to have that mental focus for hunting accuracy, because that's you providing for your family.

Even before I made it onto *American Ninja Warrior* (ANW), encouraging youth to be healthy, both physically and mentally, has been my passion—trying to be the best possible model I can. My *why* has a lot to do with that kid, the captain of my basketball team who begged and encouraged me to learn the Native Games. That kid was Axel Johnson, the one who'd beaten me up almost daily, but then pushed me to join the Games. Now a big part of what I do for kids in Alaska is suicide awareness, because over time, we've lost too many. One of them was my friend, Axel.

The way we're preventing suicide is not by telling kids to avoid it, but by telling them to confront it through positive interaction— WEIO and ANW are based on sportsmanship, camaraderie, teaching, and passing along the traditions, but most importantly, supporting one another.

I want kids to know that if they come from a broken home, like me . . . if they come from a community, like mine . . . if they're going to a dark place, like I have . . . they can still stay positive. Through Alaska Native sports, I found my lifeline in physical challenges, healthy friendships, and connection to my culture. Alaska Native sports saved my life, and they still help point the way to hope.

INTRODUCTION
PERSONAL BEST

by Tricia Nuyaqik Brown and Joni Kitmiiq Spiess

Centuries before the first Greek Olympic games took place in 776 AD, the first Alaskans from different tribal groups competed against each other in friendly "our man is stronger than your man" games. Those contests continue today, many of them unchanged in their form and purpose.

What is the human body capable of doing? If you've faced a life-or-death situation, you'd want to know that answer about your own body. Surviving in the wilderness—or worse, surviving when something goes *wrong* in the wilderness—requires physical strength and mental toughness. Could an Iñupiaq seal hunter who is stranded on the ice jump from one floe to another? Could the Athabascan moose hunter load a hundred pounds of meat on his back and then quickly get to his feet? Could the Yup'ik fisherman's hands maintain a strong grip after hours of pulling fish? Each of the Alaska Native Games emulates real-life situations like these.

In this book, you'll learn how to play centuries-old games with intriguing names, like the Eskimo Stick Pull, Ear Weight, Musk Ox Wrestling (no, you don't really wrestle the animal!), and Two-Foot High Kick. What do they require of you? Strength, balance, precision, and endurance. Mental focus. The will to challenge yourself and bring out the best in another. Exactly what's needed for survival in a harsh environment.

"It's building mental and physical abilities—just to survive, to withstand," says Brian Walker, former director of the World Eskimo-Indian Olympics (WEIO) board. Naturally, you want to encourage your competition, Brian says. "If you're gonna be out on the ice with this guy, you don't want a wimp!"

Each July since 1961, athletes have met in Fairbanks to compete at WEIO, the pinnacle of Native sports. The decades have changed, the faces have changed, but how the Games are played has not changed, thanks to elders who keep a watchful eye and ready advice on form and technique.

Indigenous peoples of every circumpolar nation independently created their own versions of testing. Some play games that aren't taught in Alaska. However, first people throughout the northern lands had certain values in common: responsibility to tribe, hard work, sharing, humor, hunter success, knowledge of family tree, patience, and honoring elders. Those values were woven into every facet of life and are reflected in these athletes.

Alaska's traditional Games require the simplest equipment, such as a tapered stick, a sealskin ball, and a string made of animal sinew. Elders say they were designed for play in small quarters, such as the sod dwellings and meeting places of long ago. Boys and girls still practice in their rooms, or in the living room, then the gym, and finally, an arena.

At WEIO, a teenager tries to maintain his stance while muscling a stick out of another man's hand in the Indian Stick Pull. The Seal Hop, or Knuckle Hop, displays the ultimate in focus and fitness as players plank their bodies and bounce forward on knuckles and toes, mimicking a hunter's stealthy approach to a seal's breathing hole in the ice.

At the Native Youth Olympics in Anchorage, a girl's eyes are focused on the handmade sealskin ball hanging from a string. Competing in the Two-Foot High Kick, she quickly trots toward her mark then leaps, snaps into a jackknife position, like a diver, and throws both feet toward the target, tagging it with a toe. She has just kicked higher than the top of her head.

"I could never do that," you might think. But with proper training, you may surprise yourself. Kids start early in Alaska, and Anchorage's public school curriculum is introducing "Indigenous Games of North America" to family nights. The Junior

Native Youth Olympics (JNYO) invites the first- through sixth-graders to compete in Anchorage each winter. In late April, top athletes from seventh to twelfth grades come to the University of Alaska, Anchorage, for the Native Youth Olympics (NYO). You don't have to be Native to compete in those contests.

WEIO in Fairbanks is the granddaddy event of them all, a grand family reunion of Alaska Natives with more than just sporting events. There's a Miss WEIO event, seal-skinning contests, regalia judging (even for baby regalia), dancing demonstrations, arts and crafts sales, and lots of feasting. Every other year, Team Alaska competes at the Arctic Winter Games (AWG) against athletes from Canada's northernmost provinces, northern Scandinavia, Russia, and Greenland. The AWG venues rotate, always in a circumpolar city.

No matter where the Games are held, above all the noise you'll hear a high note of encouragement. Sure, a sympathetic audience groans when a boy's foot just misses his goal or when a girl rocks off her feet and touches the floor. But it's the athletes themselves who raise the bar of sportsmanship as an essential cultural value. They'll circle around opponents with advice, encouragement, and their very presence in support. Some of the most prestigious awards recognize sportsmanship. It's the Native way.

World Knuckle Hop champion Rod Worl, who's medaled repeatedly since the early 1980s, says that attitude makes these Games unlike any other competitive sport. There's no trash talking another person, team, or culture.

Athletes collaborate. "It's more about competing with yourself and your personal record," Rod says. "Everybody's helping each other and everybody's teaching each other . . . and making lifelong friends through that process."

Competitive kids train with coaches, many of them record holders themselves who've grounded their own lives in sports. Nicole Johnston was a fifth-grader in Nome when a few elders gathered up some kids after church one Sunday. *Try it*, they said. Young Nicole astonished the elders when she nailed her kick on the first try. She remembers thinking, "What? It was easy." In her career, Nicole has medaled in nearly every event. A longtime coach and mentor, Nicole still competes and also crisscrosses the state organizing NYO events and saying *Try it* to this generation. Hearing a surprised kid say, "I did that!" is her greatest reward.

The youth seem most aware about how these Games can change lives. They resolve to push themselves. They tap deeper strength through friendships. They reconnect with their cultures by doing what the ancestors did. The result: healthier bodies, healthier minds, healthier spirits. Some find addictions lose their grip, thoughts of self-harm are crowded out, sadness is overcome by life with meaning and goals.

Medals, awards, and records aside, even "bragging rights" aside, it's all about pressing the limits, says Brian Walker. He sums it up this way: "You are there to better yourself and try your hardest, and help your fellow competitor do their best and try their hardest."

It's the Native way.

A successful seal hunter.
ALASKA STATE LIBRARY,
LOMEN BROTHERS
(PHOTOGRAPH COLLECTION,
1903-1920, ASL-P29-170)

v

PART I

ANCIENT GAMES AND MODERN MUSCLE

A young competitor steadies
her target ball, which was
crafted from sealskin.

ALASKAN HIGH KICK

This difficult game requires a completely upside-down posture, a one-handed handstand with a full-body stretch so the player can kick a suspended ball. With repetition, players gain endurance and strength needed to hunt wild game.

// HOW TO PLAY //

In a seated position, grab the top or bottom of one foot with the opposite hand. Your other leg is resting in a bent position. Place your free hand on the floor behind you with a straight arm. Now pull on your foot, upward, and raise your whole body upward. Stretch out that free leg until you can touch the suspended ball with any part of your foot. Keep holding the toe of that one foot the whole time; land on the same foot that kicks the ball. It's okay to hop on that foot to catch your balance. With each successful kick, the ball is moved higher for the next try.

"For Alaskan [High Kick], you have to start small," advises WEIO champion Elijah Cabinboy. "Practice positioning while seated first."

All athletes can make three attempts at all height intervals. Any missed kicks are noted and counted if the contestant qualifies for the final attempt.

// MATERIALS NEEDED //

A kick ball and a kick stand. For safety, make sure the ground is even and flat.

Tim Fields of Noorvik executes the Alaskan High Kick.

Right: David Thomas is a picture of perfect balance, while extending his left leg to touch the ball with his foot.

Raven Willoya-Williams, left, pits her strength against Yvonne Flynn.

ARM PULL

Upper-body strength is essential for hauling heavy loads of meat, gear, and supplies. This strength-testing game pits two players against each other. They begin by sitting face to face closely, with their legs overlapping on each side. One leg is over and one leg under their opponent's thighs. On the next round, leg placement is reversed.

Begin by linking opposing arms at the elbow. If your thigh is on top, you'll compete using the arm on that same side of your body. Use your free hand to reach out and grip your opponent's opposite foot on the floor. Keeping a straight back and neck, lean back and pull as you try to straighten the other person's arm. Sometimes players pull the other athlete right off the floor, or even into a standing position.

Marcus Holley of Cordova wins a round in the Arm Pull.

// MATERIALS NEEDED //

No equipment is necessary, but it's smart to do this on a soft surface.

DROP THE BOMB / AIRPLANE

Drop the Bomb requires such physical and mental discipline that only a few individuals will compete. In a place where one's survival can depend on how strong you are, this is a perfect demonstration of how stamina, physical power, and mental discipline converge to create an amazing athlete.

// HOW TO PLAY //

Begin by lying face down on the floor with arms straight out at the sides. Keep your feet together, toes down. Every muscle is taut and held in a planking position as "carriers" take hold of your stiff, straight arms at the wrists and hold up your feet with a strap around the ankles. The carriers lift you off the floor just a few inches and quickly walk as far as possible while you keep that all-muscles-engaged position, like a human airplane, facing downward, and completely stiff.

The carriers must crouch over so that you, the "airplane," are as close to the ground as possible whenever your body gives up. Their work is not easy, either. The athlete (and team) who goes the farthest is the winner.

Jeff Maupin of Barrow held a long-time record of traveling 266 feet during the 1987 WEIO.

// PLAY IT AT HOME? //

Probably not yet. Drop the Bomb is played only at WEIO and the Arctic Winter Games, and young athletes can look forward to competing in it at those senior levels.

Kyle Worl endures to gain more ground during WEIO's Drop the Bomb event.
(PHOTO BY GREG LINCOLN/DELTA DISCOVERY)

EAR PULL

Some Games are more painful than others, and the Ear Pull is one that's not meant for everyone. In fact, according to Sam Strange of Chugiak, an official, medalist, and record breaker, success in this event often depends on the ears you're born with: firm or floppy. While other family members excel at Ear Pull, it's not Sam's game. (But he does know pain. In 2016, Sam won the Four-Man Carry by walking almost 113 feet while carrying almost one-third ton of weight.)

"We tell folks to compete in this game, you need good ears, good cartilage," says Sam. "My son Seth definitely took after his mom's ears. I've got Dumbo ears."

// HOW TO PLAY //

With a set-up similar to the Arm Pull, two players sit facing each other with legs overlapping. Their hands may support them on the floor or knees. A loop of braided sinew is passed around each person's ear, connecting their heads. At the signal, they pull back until the pain is too great for one of them, or the string rolls off somebody's ear. No twisting or jerking is allowed. The best two out of three attempts wins.

Injuries do occur, and some players have cut a groove where the ear meets their head. Officials decided to change the type of sinew from a solo string to a three-string braided loop, which rolls off easier, rather than cut. Strange says some athletes have built up a callous.

// TRY IT AT HOME? //

Not recommended. Let's leave it to the pros.

Corey Olympic withstands the pain as he tries to outlast his opponent.

Leroy Shangin is a regular medalist. Competitors may not tilt their heads so their cheek bears some of the weight.
(PHOTO BY GREG LINCOLN/DELTA DISCOVERY)

EAR WEIGHT

Dealing with pain during a hunt, withstanding cold or physical pain, is part of the reality of living a subsistence lifestyle. This "pain game" combines genetics of good, firm ears with speed walking. The question is, how far can you go while carrying lead weight at the end of a braided nylon rope? Oh, and that weight is hanging from your ear.

Contestants may not tilt their heads to bear some of the weight on their cheeks. Winners are decided by the distance they travel and how much weight they carry.

In the 2011 WEIO, the amazing Homer Lord, best known for his strength achievements in Four-Man Carry and Arm Pull, endured 552 feet, 11 inches of walking while hauling sixteen pounds of lead from one ear. He took home the gold and said years of wrestling made his ears "strong."

By the 2019 WIO, Leroy Shangin of Anchorage was repeatedly landing in the top three in both Ear Pull and Ear Weight, year after year. Yet record holder Michael Paulsen of Barrow held the top spot with an unbelievable 2,886-foot, 10-inch walk.

Alaska NYO coordinator Adele Ridley embraces her grandmother, Sophie Nosthine. Both are tattooed—the elder with a traditional chin tattoo and the younger with a meaningful message.

ESKIMO STICK PULL

This game mimics the approach to a seal's breathing hole and what it takes to pull in a seal. You are the hunter creeping toward the hole. At last the seal pops its head up, and you successfully harpoon it. That will mean good meat and seal oil to share, and a sturdy hide to sew into clothes, balls (for the kicking games), and fishing floats. When the seal takes a dive, you must hang on and then steadily pull the seal back to the surface. You need strong hands, arms, and back.

// HOW TO PLAY //

Sit across from your opponent sole-to-sole with knees bent at 45 degrees. The stick should be positioned horizontally between you. Each person grips the stick with both hands. In the first round, you may grip both hands at the center of the stick; your opponent's hands will be to the left and right of yours. Placement will reverse in the next round. Be sure to stay in the seated position. To be safe, keep your wrists and arms straight, and your neck should be aligned with your straight back. At GO, try to pull the stick from the other person's hands. Twisting or jerking is not allowed. Each pair will pull three times. The best two out of three rounds wins.

// TRY IT AT HOME //

All you need is a foam yoga mat as you sit facing each other. Use a 1 ¼-inch dowel that's 20 inches long. That's competition size. Make sure there's plenty of space for a safety zone around you.

A Valdez athlete gives it his all.

FOUR-MAN CARRY

The strongest of the strong get the spotlight in this game that feels like you're hauling a cow moose (or small grand piano) around a gym.

// HOW TO PLAY //

At the start line, the athlete crouches while four young men encircle his neck—one in front, one in back, and one on each side. When he stands, the men are dangling with their knees bent. Now the long walk begins while he carries as much as six hundred pounds. In a game that's measured by distance, not time, speed walking helps. When the athlete is done, he's done, often collapsing to the floor, so those guys must quickly release and hop away to avoid being crushed.

The late "Big Bob" Aiken of Barrow stood tall in this game for years. Size matters, and he was six feet four. Then there's Sam Strange, who says, "I don't look very muscular. I'm only five feet ten and I've medaled almost every year I've entered, usually third. You're carrying six hundred pounds—definitely compresses the spine. It just wipes you out."

Those "carry-ees" must be in good shape, too, Strange says. "It's tiring for them; they're having to hang on, getting squished and chunked. The guys collapse, and they fall on the carry-ees. They get beat."

Stanley Riley of Anaktuvuk Pass set a new world record in 2019 by walking 334 feet, 3½ inches—more than two laps around the WEIO gym floor. "Four-man carry is crazy," Stan told a reporter. "It's like you go to this point where your knees are wobbling and you see sparkles . . . you don't get enough oxygen."

// TRY IT AT HOME? //

Not for growing kids. This one's for the masters.

Four young men cling to Robert Strick's neck in the Four-Man Carry.

Caitlyn Pickett gingerly steps along a greased spruce pole.

GREASED POLE WALK

It's hard enough to cross a log over a stream, but try it when it's slimy and wet, and you can imagine what it's like for contestants in this event. They grease it up beautifully before the contest. There's lots of big arm waving as players just try to stay standing and take small steps. No sliding.

// HOW TO PLAY //

Take off your shoes and find your balance at one end of a horizontal log that's been greased. At GO, carefully inch to the other end without falling off. It's harder than it looks. In competition, spotters walk along each side to grab you if you fall (or is that *when* you fall?).

AwaLuk Nichols is a middle-school girl with long ancestry in Alaska's northwestern region. She's descended from King Island on her mom's side, and from White Mountain / Golovin on her dad's side. In 2019, AwaLuk entered the Greased Pole Walk in the NYO Games and, thanks to lots of training and excellent balance, she placed second.

HEAD PULL / NECK PULL

Upper-body strength is challenged in this face-to-face power struggle. Bound to your opponent by a strap, you pull that person in your direction using your neck, shoulders, and arms.

// HOW TO PLAY //

Athletes lie on the floor and face each other with their arms straight like a push-up, and bodies in a plank position. A two-inch-wide leather strap measuring three feet long is placed around their necks, linking their heads. The goal is to pull the strap off your opponent's head or pull him or her toward you and over a marked line two feet behind you. As with other pulling games, jerking or twisting is not allowed.

During play, the athlete's knees can touch the ground, but players cannot lie down.

Gary Hull, right, attempts to pull the strap off his opponent.

Kyle Worl, right, tries to wrench a greased stick from his rival.

INDIAN STICK PULL

The Alaska Indian tribal groups include the Athasbascan, Tlingit, Haida, Eyak, and Tsimshian. Like all of Alaska's indigenous people, working together and sharing has ensured survival for all. And fish has always been an important part of the menu, year-round, whether it's eaten fresh, dried, smoked, or otherwise stored to enjoy during the cold winter months. The Indian Stick Pull simulates pulling slippery fish from the net or fish wheel, quickly and efficiently, which takes coordination and endurance. "The Indian Stick Pull is more about technique," says expert Sam Strange. "Nothing to do with strength."

// HOW TO PLAY //

Participants stand side by side, but facing opposite directions, with feet at shoulder's width. The long side of their opposing feet are touching, pinkie toe to heel. Each takes hold of a greased, tapered stick that's placed between them horizontally. The goal is to pull the stick from the other person's hand. At Native Youth Olympics, rules state that players cannot raise the stick above shoulder height of the shortest player. It's a pushing and pulling game, but jerking is encouraged. Pulling when the other guy is expecting pushing is a good trick, too. The one who pulls the "fish" from their opponent's hand is the winner.

// TRY IT AT HOME //

Just for fun, make it harder. Instead of a stick, use a toy fish and coat it with baby oil to make it nice and slimy like a fish.

KNEEL JUMP

A tough competitor for years, Brian Walker is an Ingalik Athabascan, raised in the remote village of Anvik, where moose hunters need a strong back and legs to pack out their load of game meat. He's carried plenty, and he's competed in the difficult Four-Man Carry, a true test of power.

The Kneel Jump demonstrates how the hunter's leg strength and speed gets him or her from a kneeling position to launching forward and standing, but without pushing off the floor with their hands.

Apaay Campbell made a significant win in 2013, when she met her goal of beating her own mother's twenty-year record. How? "I use a lot of breathing techniques," Apaay said, "like concentrating on a goal spot on the floor, strengthening abdominal muscles, and staying fit all year round."

// HOW TO PLAY //

Begin by kneeling upright with your heels under your bottom. With a straight back, swing your arms forward and leap up onto your feet without touching your hands on the floor. The goal is to jump as far forward as possible from that starting position. The jump is measured from the start line. The best of three jumps is recorded.

// MATERIALS NEEDED //

It's best to perform this on hardwood gym floors. Carpet can cause skin burns.

First-grader Henry Stille shows perfect form in the Kneel Jump.

KNUCKLE HOP / SEAL HOP

Stamina as well as arm and core strength are needed while traveling or hunting in the backcountry, and this game demonstrates how generations of Alaska Natives maintained it. This is one of those events that makes the audience hold its breath. Athletes ignore pain as they repeatedly pound their knuckles into the hard floor while traveling forward.

// HOW TO PLAY //

In a face-down plank position, balance only on your closed fist and toes. For young teens, fingers are tightly curled into their flat palm that's against the floor. Maintaining a flat back and straight arms throughout the challenge, you'll create a bounce effect using foot and arm strength to hop forward. Distance is measured from the start line to the end in a straight-line course. If you make it to the end, you may cross that line with your fingertips, turn, and head back to the start line. If form is not maintained in the plank position, you'll be asked to stop.

Hand position varies by age. The junior competitors at JNYO can use a flat hand instead of knuckles; at NYO, the palm is flat, but fingers are curled at the fingertips; for the seniors, they travel with stiff wrists and full-on downward fists. The big knuckles contact the floor.

In 1988, Rod Worl set the record at 191 feet, 10 inches in the Knuckle Hop. It remains untouched.

// MATERIALS NEEDED //

A measuring tape and a wooden gym floor (something other than carpet).

Young competitors use a flat palm during this event. Adults who use bare knuckles sometimes take weeks to heal.

KYLE WORL, GOLD MEDALIST:

The first time I ever did Knuckle Hop was on a hardwood surface. I remember that pain and thinking that I might never be able to do this. My father holds the world record, and that's a lot of pressure. Over the years, I pushed myself, and I slowly got better at it. I slowly learned pain endurance, that mental strength. It was a lot of encouragement from fellow athletes and my dad's coaching. I've been successful in Knuckle Hop and placed gold several times. My personal best is 167'—still 30 feet off from my dad's record.

I coach here in Juneau. My athletes compete right next to me. I always have to remind them of where I started. It did take me years of practice and training. I do most all the Games, but I love the Knuckle Hop because it is such a challenge. Anything that's a challenge, the success feels even better.

It's about pushing your limits. When you get down on the floor and compete, and you start to feel your body wants to give in with fatigue, your muscles are burning, your body is telling you to give in and you don't have anything left, but the game is to keep going and pushing those physical limits. You get this amazing adrenalin rush, and the crowd—your community, your family, your friends—they're all cheering you on, and it becomes just deafening. They're yelling, they're screaming your name. You can't hear words—they're almost a little drowned out—but it all becomes this one big cheer that's pushing you to keep going. That cheer is working against the voice in your head telling you that your body is done. It's really amazing.

Nick Hanson's battered hands were still healing several weeks after the 2019 WEIO Knuckle Hop competition.
(PHOTO BY TRICIA BROWN)

The modern-day blanket toss event (top) contrasts with a century-old photo from Barrow showing the blanket toss during the spring whaling celebration called Nalukataq.
(HISTORIC PHOTO FROM THE ALASKA STATE LIBRARY, REV. SAMUEL SPRIGGS PHOTOGRAPHS, ASL-P320-36)

NALUKATAQ
(BLANKET TOSS)

Bicycling your feet while high in the air above a sealskin blanket is the idea of good fun for Alaska's Iñupiat. Traditionally, Blanket Toss was a way to signal a successful hunt as well as a celebratory part of the whaling festival known in northern Alaska as Nalukataq (Iñupiaq for "blanket toss"). At the big outdoor picnic along the Arctic Ocean, the successful whaling crew's captain is usually the first to step onto the tough sealskin blanket. Standing at the center, the captain is surrounded by a ring of "pullers" holding rope handles that lift and droop the blanket in rhythm. And then, all at once, the pullers pop the blanket up, and the captain flies high. Other captains and their wives step up next, throwing out candy to the watching crowd while airborne.

// HOW TO PLAY //

In competitions, it's all about height, style, and landing. The favorites will maintain their upright body position, with good form and the occasional flip, keeping control of their balance while airborne. Landing squarely on your feet is a must.

One of the best known in the sport is Reggie Joule of Kotzebue, who never failed to inspire with his powerful jumps during the 1970s and 1980s. In his senior years, he's served as a statesman representing his region. A crowd at WEIO's fiftieth anniversary was delighted to see this skilled elder take to the blanket again. Reggie won a silver medal (to match his silver ponytail).

// MYTH BUSTING //

Blanket Toss was not used for spotting whales. Whalers actually stood on the shore's highest pressure ridges of ice, using binoculars to carefully locate a spouting whale. You can't do that when you're flying through the air!

Jens Irelan and Kyle Clark, cousins from the
Nome-Beltz Nanook Team, warm up and prepare
to compete at NYO in Anchorage.

Louella Tumulak strains to tap the fur ball.

ONE-FOOT HIGH KICK

Like the other kicking games, this one measures agility, precision, and leg strength, all needed for survival in Bush Alaska, from ancient times to today.

// HOW TO PLAY //

Begin with a running start toward a kick ball suspended above you. Swing your arms to gain momentum as you jump off the ground with both feet. Only one foot goes the full distance to kick the suspended ball with any part of the foot. Then you must land on the same foot that kicked the ball. If you lose balance upon landing, it's okay to hop.

Scorekeepers count all attempts to kick the ball. With each successful strike, the ball is moved up four inches higher for the next attempt. But if you miss, it's counted against you. If two players are tied for the same height, the person with the most misses loses. Or there's a kick-off to award the win.

At the 2013 NYO, Tim Field of Noorvik broke a record in this event held by Jesse Frankson of Point Hope. He had set it at WEIO nine years earlier. "Records are meant to be broken," Tim said just before stepping up to kick the ball hanging 117 inches above the floor. He beat Frankson's amazing kick by 1 inch.

// TRY IT AT HOME //

If you don't have a suitable leather or sealskin ball for trying this game, begin by using a whiffle ball hanging from the ceiling, and keep it low at first. Put plenty of room around the kicking ball so you have a safety zone.

// MATERIALS NEEDED //

Kick ball and kick stand with space enough for approach, kicking, and landing safely.

THE SPIRITUAL CONNECTION

When Sheila Randazzo was a little girl, her cousins came into Nome for the Games, and she was an excited spectator. "It helped as a child to affirm who I was as a Native young person," she remembers. "Back then, I thought I wanted to play Games when I got older." And she did, entering as many Games as she could in high school, and medaling in Toe Kick, One-Foot High Kick, and One-Arm Reach, among others. She even won the Sportsmanship Award as a teenager. And Sheila became the wife and mother of two other famous competitors: Brian Randazzo Sr. and Brian Randazzo Jr.

Like so many other Alaska Natives, Sheila confirms that competing holds much deeper meaning than just who wins and who loses:

"It was a big part of my youth in high school. It helped me to feel really proud of being Alaska Native. Understanding self, coming to terms with who you are as a young person. It affirmed value and worth and honor.

"Our Games, our dance, our values, those are all things we're grasping for, to help us affirm our worth, our importance in our society. In our culture, we're trying to hold onto our traditional ways of life and our values, the way we cooperate with one another and support one another. We're still trying to hold onto that in the Native Games.

"There's something about our Games, our dance, our way of life, that helps to fill a void. I think that void is just feeling proud of yourself.

"There's something spiritual about the Native Games—it also affirms that Native people are good, are positive, are proud. We have such a stigma, still. There's so far to go, still. Young people are still yearning for some things to hold onto to make them feel proud."

Aphanasia Kvasnikoff of Nanwalek shows the sequence and form of this difficult event.

All are welcome to join the dancing
during an invitational song.

ONE-HAND REACH

The balance and power required for this game is phenomenal, as you must arrange your body to balance over a single hand that's flat on the floor. With one hand supporting your weight, the other reaches upward to touch a suspended ball.

Bernard "Spiderman" Clark once stretched out 81 ½ inches—the wingspan of a Golden Eagle—to win this event. What competing has taught him: "Learning what you can accomplish is one of the best things in life. The next best is failure. It is not the attempt that is the most difficult, it is failure and getting back up. That is why a goal you set should be *improving* **and not** *striving for perfection.*"

// HOW TO PLAY //

Place one hand on the ground with fingers spread wide. Now lean forward onto that hand while tucking your elbow under your hip. Curl your legs to the side to center your weight over that hand. Now, while balancing, turn your head and focus on the ball above you. Use your free hand to reach upward and touch the ball with any part of your hand. Each competitor gets three attempts to touch the ball, and it's moved higher with each successful try. Missed attempts are counted, and the athlete with the fewest misses advances to the next round or wins.

As an alternate way to balance, a bridged hand or a closed fist can be used instead of a flat hand if the athlete shows he or she can maintain control before, during, and after the attempt.

// MATERIALS NEEDED //

A kick ball and kick stand.

Auktweena (Caitlin) Tozier of Nome carefully balances on one arm while reaching upward.

SCISSOR BROAD JUMP

Another game that recalls the importance of survival skills, the Scissor Broad Jump emulates a person jumping from ice floe to ice floe in spring, when hunters are out looking for seals and the icebergs are spreading far apart. How far can you hop?

A favored emcee at the Games for many years was Robert "Big Bob" Aiken Jr., who's remembered for his humorous narration. If a Scissor Broad Jump player lost his balance and sat, Big Bob's big voice would fill the room: "Uuup! He fell in the water!"

// HOW TO PLAY //

Begin by standing with your feet as wide as your shoulders. Now jump far forward from the start line, leading with the right foot. Don't stop! Carry on that forward momentum, immediately crossing your left leg behind the right and landing on the left foot. Without pausing, lead with your right foot, and jump forward as far as possible to land on both feet. You must maintain balance at the end of the jump. No sitting down. The distance from the start line to landing is measured, and everyone gets three tries. The longest of the three jumps is recorded.

// MATERIALS NEEDED //

A rubberized or wooden gym floor and clean shoes. If the athlete chooses to, he or she can jump barefoot.

Cordova's Gunnar Davis, a fifth-grader, demonstrates the complicated steps of the Scissor Broad Jump.

TOE KICK

According to tradition, this game kept people light on their toes and helped build the speed and agility needed to hunt safely on the ice.

// HOW TO PLAY //

Stand with your feet together behind a line, then leap forward as far as possible. However, before landing, you must use the toes of both feet to kick a stick that's lying horizontally in the path ahead. In one continuous motion, tag it with both toes, making it spin backward, before landing on both feet. Hopping on both feet afterward to maintain balance is okay, but you must stay upright. The stick has to show measurable evidence that it has spun backward. With each successful try, the stick is placed another four inches away from the start line until you can no longer make contact. The kick counts only if the athlete kicks the stick without landing on it. Each player gets three tries to kick the stick at given distances.

// MATERIALS NEEDED //

A one-inch dowel cut to one foot long. Play on a flat, clean surface.

// TRY IT AT HOME //

For fun, instead of the regulation dowel size, practice the game using a pencil or a pool noodle.

Toe Kick competitors know that timing and balance are essential for executing this game.

TWO-FOOT HIGH KICK

Generations ago, the Two-Foot High Kick was used to send long-distance messages from an Iñupiat whaling crew to a village, saying they'd caught a whale. The sight of this kick generated a happy "Aarigaa!" or "Yay! Very good!" The signal also said it was time for the villagers to get ready—lots of work was ahead. The whole community prepared to pull in the whale, assembling what they needed to butcher the animal on the shore ice. Everyone gathered to help. Some of the whale was shared right away; later, more meat and *muktuk* (the skin and blubber) would be divided into portions for every family who wanted some.

// HOW TO PLAY //

A ball is suspended from the ceiling or an apparatus. You stand with feet together and eyes on the ball, then run toward the target. Quickly stop then jump upward into a pike position to kick the ball, making sure that your feet stay even with each other as you kick. You must land back on two feet. It's okay to hop on both feet afterward for balance. The kicking ball is raised higher with each successful attempt.

// MATERIALS NEEDED //

A sealskin or leather ball that's suspended from the ceiling or an apparatus.

Austin Yanalcheen S'awdaan successfully connects with the kick ball.

An athlete dangles from a bar with his wrist taking the brunt of his weight.

WRIST CARRY

People-watching at this endurance event is almost as much fun as watching the athlete. The faces of the viewers are so expressive as they sympathize with the contestants' hard work.

// HOW TO PLAY //

Another grueling test of strength and endurance, the Wrist Carry requires you to hook one wrist over a pole from below, so you're hanging by your wrist. Teammates on each side quickly walk or run forward, carrying the pole while you curl up your legs and feet to stay off the floor. The one who goes the farthest before giving out is the winner.

Lindsay Merculief hung from her wrist while moving the length of almost two football fields! She won the girls' Wrist Carry in 2006 by traveling 662 feet, 4 inches. Her best advice: "Do your planks! The more planks, the farther the distance!"

PART II

JUST AS FIERCE, BUT NEARLY FORGOTTEN

Over time, a few Games were shelved until WEIO leadership decided to resurrect some old favorites for its fiftieth anniversary year. They were so popular that the competitors didn't want to put them back in the archives and asked they be rotated into the schedule. Some are performed simply for demonstration.

Wearing a miniature fancy parka, this baby delights in attention from mom. Along with its athletic events, WEIO draws competitors in regalia sewing, muktuk-eating, and fish-cutting.

The ultimate planking exercise engages every muscle for Seth Strange. This event replicates the strength needed for hauling large marine and land mammals after a successful hunt.

BENCH REACH

This game is now played at WEIO every other year, but it was created to help increase the core strength needed to hunt and then haul moose, caribou, walrus, or seal meat back home.

// HOW TO PLAY //
Kneel on a padded bench with your knees just at the edge. A sturdy helper sits on your lower legs to counterbalance as your lean forward and put an object on the floor as far out as possible. No extra support from the athlete's hands or another person is allowed. In three tries, you reach out, hold your position, and place the object. Distance is measured from the bench.

// TO PREPARE //
As with all the events, safety is the largest concern. To prepare, stretch out the large muscles of the back, arms, and core.

// TRY IT AT HOME //
Practice with the knees resting on the floor behind a marked spot.

CARIBOU WRESTLING / MUSK OX (OR MOOSE!) WRESTLING

Like the biggest males in caribou or musk oxen herds, people in Alaska's remote villages traditionally tested one another physically to see who was strongest. This game mimics an animal that is fighting for mating rights or to establish itself as herd leader.

// HOW TO PLAY //

In this display of strength, two players are on their hands and knees, each taking a turn at pushing the opposing player out of an established area. For Caribou Wrestling, you face each other on hands and knees, placing the top of your head under the flat area of your opponent's shoulder. Now start pushing as hard as you can to get the other guy moving backward. For Musk Ox or Moose Wrestling, you begin forehead-to-forehead in this pushing contest. Using strong legs and back, you must force your opponent backward and behind a line.

// TO PREPARE //

Make sure that your neck and back are warmed up and stretched. To compete safely, the neck area and upper body needs to move freely, so neck rolls and upper-body stretches are a must. The floor should be clean and uncluttered. For equipment, all you need is a half-inch-thick floor mat.

// TRY IT AT HOME //

Choose to be a caribou, moose, or a musk ox fighting its own kind. On your hands and knees, face another kid in the same position. Keep your neck and back in alignment. If you can push your opponent out of the circle, you win.

Seth Strange, right, and Robert Ahmasuk ready themselves to push each other out of bounds.

For Fish Hook, Robert Ahmasuk, right, and Seth Strange each "hooks" his opponent, pulling until he turns his head.

FISH HOOK

Another one of the "pain games," Fish Hook requires a high tolerance for discomfort.

// HOW TO PLAY //

Two players begin by kneeling next to each other, shoulder to shoulder and facing the same direction. Using your inside arms, reach around the back of your opponent's head and hook your index finger into the corner of his or her lip. At the signal, begin pulling, just like you're hooking a fish, until somebody finally gives up. Don't be surprised if your eyes spontaneously shed tears.

Robert Ahmasuk demonstrates the game of Nose Pull. The win goes to whoever endures the longest.

NOSE PULL

Nose Pull is similar to the Ear Pull in that all you need is a dense string. Compressing the nose can cause tears to flow, and in competition, there are lots of sympathy groans from the audience. Both games represent the pain of frostbite, says long-time competitor and mentor Sam Strange. "Nose Pull is just for demonstration now, not competitive."

// HOW TO PLAY //

Opponents stand or sit back to back, and a tightly braided loop of sinew string encircles both of their heads. The string is carefully placed at the tip of each person's nose. At the signal, they lean away from each other and the string does its evil work, digging in and compressing their noses. Naturally, there's lots of grimacing in this game. Whoever gives up first has lost the match.

"The nose can turn black and blue over time," Sam says. Yep, it's just like frostbite.

A 2009 NYO official sports a T-shirt
recognizing decades of dedication to
sustaining the Games.

OLD LADIES' GAME

Humor is a hallmark of everyday life for the Natives of Alaska, crossing all tribal lines, and this game always generates lots of laughter, especially from the players.

// HOW TO PLAY //
The game begins with two "mature" women who loop a leather strap behind their necks and under their thighs just above the knee.

They start out by lying on their sides on the ground, looking like bound hostages.

Without using their hands, the women must wiggle around to get into an upright position, and then try to knock over the other lady. Everybody's laughing, especially at the end, when the champion finishes by sitting on her downed opponent!

Shelby and Seth Strange show how the Old Ladies' Game always ends in laughter.

SWING KICK

Like so many Games, this one really requires good balance and strength in every part of the body. Now that it's been reintroduced, it's once again popular among competitors.

// HOW TO PLAY //

A leather strap measuring one-inch wide and about two feet in diameter is looped behind the neck and the knees. You must balance on your hands, take your feet off the floor, and then extend your legs to kick a suspended ball. The tricky part is beginning and ending with your feet off the floor.

A top competitor in many events, Kyle Worl of Juneau set a world record at the 2016 WEIO, balancing on his hands and swing kicking a ball set at sixty-three inches. One reporter said Kyle looked like he was "performing a contortionist's act."

// TRY IT AT HOME? //

Not typically recommended for early elementary students.

His legs bound to his neck, Seth Strange balances on his hands while swinging his legs to kick the ball.

THE GREAT ONES

STUNNING MOMENTS AND
UNFORGETTABLE COMPETITORS
WHO **MADE** AND **BROKE RECORDS**.

The aurora borealis dances
above a boreal forest.
The northern lights are a
source of many ancestral
stories throughout the
circumpolar north.

ROBERT "BIG BOB" AIKEN JR. OF BARROW

At six-foot-four and nearly five hundred pounds at his top-end weight, the late Big Bob was a giant in many ways, loved for his quick wit, his encouragement of other athletes, and his example of insisting that methods stay exactly as they've been for centuries. Sensational video of his 1979 Four-Man Carry performance at WEIO shows the big man easily striding forward with a "necklace" of four men hanging with locked arms around his neck and shoulders. In retirement, he remained a favorite, joking as he emceed events. One of his favorite sayings was "A man has got to know his limits."

BRIAN RANDAZZO SR. AND BRIAN RANDAZZO JR. OF ANCHORAGE

Any fan who follows WEIO or NYO history recognizes the name Brian Randazzo Sr. A superstar athlete, he routinely medaled in an array of events, especially in the One- and Two-Foot High Kicks. Brian Sr. remains all-time champion in the Two-Foot High Kick at eight feet, eight inches. Then his son grew up and joined the fun. At nineteen, in his very first year of WEIO competition, Brian Jr. medaled in several events and took third in the Two-Foot High Kick. Brian Jr. would go on to land his personal best jump in the 2011 Native Youth Olympics at eight feet, five inches above the floor—a foot taller than the tallest NBA player in history. Brian Sr. had stepped out of competition in 1999, and did not reenter until 2011, when both Brians fought each other in the semifinals of Indian Stick Pull. Junior finished second; Senior finished third. Both men are esteemed as among the best in the history of the Games.

Brian Sr. celebrates at the 1986 Arctic Winter Games.
(ALASKA STATE LIBRARY, ARCTIC WINTER GAMES TEAM ALASKA, 1967-, ASL-P399-0828)

Like his father, Brian Jr. excelled in traditional sports.
(PHOTO BY GREG LINCOLN/ DELTA DISCOVERY)

BRIAN WALKER OF ANVIK AND EAGLE RIVER

With a long list of achievements in strength Games like Stick Pull and Arm Pull, Brian Walker also holds a place in the books as the man who toppled the long-standing record of "Big Bob" Aiken in the Four-Man Carry. Aiken later joked that Brian had "forced him into retirement." In 1992, Brian plodded 156 feet while carrying six hundred pounds of humans hanging around his neck. How did he manage? His answer speaks of stamina from the subsistence hunter's perspective: "Traditionally, you had to keep going. If you didn't keep going, you didn't eat or drink. You'd starve." A high school educator, Brian continues to mentor and coach athletes, and serves in WEIO leadership. He remains a formidable opponent in the strength games.

A Kotzebue Democrat, Reggie served in Alaska politics for decades.
(ALASKA STATE LIBRARY, ASL PORTRAIT FILE, ASL-JOULE-REGGIE-2)

REGGIE JOULE SR. OF KOTZEBUE

For nearly two decades, Reggie Joule was king of the Blanket Toss, earning ten gold medals at WEIO for his powerful, yet graceful jumps. His golden ulu in the 1974 Arctic Winter Games was Alaska's first medal. Over time he earned twenty medals for the Arm Pull, Two-Foot High Kick, Greased Pole Walk, and more. Ever an encourager, Reggie even offered tips to those who bested him as they entered their next round. From 1997 to 2012, Reggie represented District 40 in the Alaska State Legislature, and followed that with a three-year stint as mayor of the Northwest Arctic Borough. He returned to the blanket for WEIO's fiftieth anniversary in 2011, earning a silver. Reggie was inducted into the Alaska Sports Hall of Fame in 2010.

Ben received NYO's first Lifetime Achievement Award in 2018.
(BOB HALLINEN/ANCHORAGE DAILY NEWS)

BEN SNOWBALL OF STEBBINS AND ANCHORAGE

In the early 1970s, this Yup'ik man, a former muktuk-eating champion at WEIO, helped launch the Native Youth Olympics. As an elder in the early 1990s, he joined the effort to establish the Junior Native Youth Olympics. A sculptor, drum maker, and former NYO official, he was awarded NYO's first Lifetime Achievement Award at the 2018 Games, and passed away just a few months later. He is remembered by many for his easygoing ways of teaching and leading. Adhering to the traditions surrounding the Games was all-important. One competitor remembered, "Ben actually drew pictures of how to do the Games."

NICOLE JOHNSTON OF NOME AND ANCHORAGE

In 1989, the five feet tall Nicole Johnston actually kicked a ball at six feet, six inches in the Two-Foot High Kick, earning not only a gold medal, but a record that stood for twenty-five years. One of the most decorated athletes in Native Games history, Nicole has taken home more than one hundred medals from a variety of events. At Nicole's induction into the Alaska Sports Hall of Fame in 2017, journalist Beth Bragg noted, "The medals and the records made Johnston famous. Her commitment to sharing and preserving the Games made her special, a torchbearer who passes the flame with grace and generosity." The former chair of WEIO, Johnston is NYO's head official, organizing Games, coaching, and mentoring the next generations.

From competitor to coach, official, mentor, and friend, Nicole has done it all.
(RIGHT: COURTESY ALASKA SPORTS HALL OF FAME)

Rod Worl
(PHOTO BY BRENNAN CAIN/
THE EYAK CORP.)

Kyle Worl

ROD WORL AND KYLE WORL OF JUNEAU

After repeatedly breaking his own Knuckle Hop record during the 1980s, in 1988, Rod Worl nailed 191 feet, 10 inches, a world record that remains unbroken. A top wrestler in college, Rod specialized in the strength games, especially Kneel Jump and Drop the Bomb. Through the years, Rod medaled in many events, then his kids joined him, including Kyle Worl. Having an amazing athlete for a parent doesn't guarantee success. However, there's greatness in this father-son duo. Kyle didn't begin competing until he was a high school senior. During the next ten years, he medaled in many events and edged closer to his father's Knuckle Hop record, but didn't surpass it . . . yet. Kyle jokes: "I keep in shape, I go to the gym, I practice. I did a push-up challenge before my competition. I did twelve thousand push-ups in sixty days, and I did the Knuckle Hop every single day, and it STILL wasn't enough to beat my dad's record!" Kyle coaches NYO athletes from Southeast Alaska, a region that's rebuilding teams of talented kids after a long absence from the Games.

GREG NOTHSINE
OF ANCHORAGE

Greg Nothsine may live in Anchorage, but he's rooted in the Iñupiat communities of Nome and Wales. Still, Greg's work in the Native Sobriety Movement and the traditional Games has kept him truly rooted. A champion or former champion of the Two-Foot High Kick, Arm Pull, Toe Kick, Indian Stick Pull, and Alaskan High Kick, Greg's hills-and-valleys life journey inspires others who are struggling with addiction or trying to overcome a plateau in their sport. He's been there, and he made it. Greg is also credited with founding the dance group Kingikimiut (people of the high bluff), the original name for Wales, his mother's village. By working toward athletic goals and through his dance group, Greg has restored connections that alcohol had destroyed. He remains a highly regarded athlete who loves to encourage kids.

ACKNOWLEDGMENTS

Thank you to Chugach Alaska Corporation for your financial support of the photographic undertaking for this book.

Warm thanks to my creative partners and friends. It's been a pleasure collaborating with you, Joni and Roy. Thank you Nate Bauer and Krista West of the University of Alaska Press for your wonderful support and guidance. Also, I'm grateful to Nicole Johnston, Nick Hanson, Brian Walker, Rod and Kyle Worl, and so many other awesome athletes who helped my understanding. Finally, thank you, dear family, for your love and patience even when I shooed you out of my office.
    T.B.

Since it is said that a picture is worth a thousand words, there is no amount of gratitude I could ever express to the countless athletes I photographed through the years, and to the many more, whose dedication to Native Youth Olympics and World Eskimo-Indian Olympics fulfilled many a dream. My sincere thanks to Sheri Buretta and Chugach Alaska Corporation for financial support of my photographic efforts. Also, thank you, Sam Strange, Lindsy Townsend, Caela Nielsen, Erin and Hailey Colgrove, Nick and Sarah Tiedeman, Bob Waldrop, Gordon Howell, Nicole Johnston, David Chanar, Brennan Cain/Eyak Corporation, and Greg Lincoln/Delta Discovery for your friendship, heartwarming support and tolerance of my last-minute requests. Finally, my deepest thanks to Scooter Bentson for being my light along this journey, and to my children, Hannah and Ben, for defining my purpose in life.
    R.C.

I would like to thank our ancestors who were adaptive to their environment, and for their creativity in designing meaningful ways for us to keep our bodies and minds strong.

Thank you to my family, especially my husband Ben for always understanding my vision and for supporting me in my efforts to achieve them. To my son Robert for allowing me to teach him the Games, and for Alexander, may you appreciate them for years to come.

Thank you to all of the dedicated coaches in the State of Alaska and around the Circumpolar North who give daily to our children and are helping to ensure that these Games are practiced. Thank you for working tirelessly and for your love of the Games.

To Brian Walker, who displays humility and humor, and is a wonderful role model for all who meet him. To the Irelan Family of Nome—Asaaluk, Hank, Marilyn, Jens, and Kutuq—for always being there as a second family when I was coaching in Nome. Hank and his unorthodox yet high-level training practices helped generate the greatest of our athletes' potential. To Sheila Randazzo for inspiring so many and for her dedication to the Games.

Thank you to all who have contributed in any way to the book project. To Sam, Seth, and Shelby Strange for taking photos with us. And to Casey Ferguson for going the extra mile for our beautiful cover shot.
    J.S.

MORE INFORMATION

The World Eskimo-Indian Olympics have been conducted in Fairbanks since 1961 and continues to showcase the power and endurance, as well as the mental discipline, required of Native athletes in ancient competitions. Learn more at www.weio.org.

The Arctic Winter Games celebrated its fiftieth anniversary in 2020 when athletes gathered in Whitehorse, Yukon Territory, for its biennial competition. "Arctic Winter Games brings our Circumpolar World closer together," their site states. "Strengthening and showcasing our communities and providing our young people an International Games opportunity to participate, showcase their talent and share in the joy of Sport." For more, visit www.arcticwintergames.org.

The NYO Games, also known as the Native Youth Olympics, are a favorite for Anchorage residents and visitors who come in droves to watch each April. Hosted by the Cook Inlet Tribal Council, hundreds of athletes, their supporters, and fans converge in Alaska's biggest city following a year of preparation. Ten events are highlighted during the NYO Games, and all students in the seventh to twelfth grades are welcome to compete. The Junior NYO Games, for first- through sixth-grade children, are held in Anchorage for three days each February. JNYO and NYO are open to any athlete, regardless of ethnicity. Search for NYO Games on the www.citci.org website.

Nicole Johnston's collection of sealskin balls shows how skin-sewers may choose sheared, shaved, or natural fur.

Published by
University of Alaska Press
P.O. Box 756240
Fairbanks, AK 99775-6240

Cover and interior design by 590 Design.

FRONT COVER: Along a snowy bench overlooking Cook Inlet, Casey Ferguson maintains exquisite form in the Alaskan High Kick.

BACK COVER: Shelby Strange leaps from a walrus skin in her demonstration of the Two-Foot High Kick.

Experimentation with the athletic events described in this book is at the reader's own risk. The authors and publisher are not responsible for any injuries resulting from trying the events described here.

Library of Congress Cataloging in Publication Data
Names: Brown, Tricia, author. | Spiess, Joni, author. | Corral, Roy, photographer
Title: Alaska Native Games and How to Play Them: Twenty-five Contests that Survived the Ages / Tricia Nuyaqik Brown and Joni Kitmiiq Spiess; photography by Roy Corral; foreword by Nick Iligutchiak Hanson.
Description: Fairbanks: University of Alaska Press, 2020. | Includes index. | Summary: "In this book, you'll learn how to play centuries-old games with intriguing names, like the Eskimo Stick Pull, Ear Weight, Musk Ox Wrestling (no, you don't really wrestle the animal!), and Two-Foot High Kick. What do they require of you? Strength, balance, precision, and endurance. Mental focus. The will to challenge yourself and bring out the best in another. Exactly what's needed for survival in a harsh environment"—Provided by publisher.
Identifiers: LCCN 2020001743 (print) | LCCN 2020001744 (e-book) | ISBN 9781602234185 (cloth) | ISBN 9781602234192 (e-book)
Subjects: LCSH: Indians of North America—Games—Alaska.
Classification: LCC E98.G2 B76 2020 (print) | LCC E98.G2 (e-book) | DDC 979.004/97—dc23
LC record available at https://lccn.loc.gov/2020001743
LC ebook record available at https://lccn.loc.gov/2020001744

Printed in Canada